In Troubled Times,
Looking Forward With Hope To . . .

HEAVEN
My Father's House

ANNE GRAHAM LOTZ

Foreword by BILLY GRAHAM

W PUBLISHING GROUP™

www.wpublishinggroup.com

A Division of Thomas Nelson, Inc.
www.ThomasNelson.com

HEAVEN: MY FATHER'S HOUSE
Copyright © 2001 by Anne Graham Lotz.

Published by W Publishing Group, a Division of Thomas Nelson, Inc.,
P.O. Box 141000, Nashville, Tennessee 37214.

W Publishing Group books may be purchased in bulk for educational,
business, fund-raising, or sales promotional use. For information, please
e-mail SpecialMarkets@ThomasNelson.com.

Published in association with the literary agency of Alive
Communications, Inc., 7680 Goddard Street, Suite 200,
Colorado Springs, Colorado, 80920.

Scripture quotations used in this book are from the Holy Bible,
New International Version (NIV). Copyright © 1973, 1978, 1984
International Bible Society. Used by permission
of Zondervan Bible Publishers.

Some of the material in this book has been
adapted from *A Vision of His Glory.*

ISBN 0-8499-0699-7 (sc)
ISBN 0-8499-1748-4 (hc)

Printed in the United States of America.
05 06 07 08 09 RRD 5 4 3 2 1

To the dying

and

To all who are facing the future
with a troubled heart

∞

Anne Graham Lotz   4-6-08
Naval Academy Chapel
"Hope Thats Anchored"
                  John 14:1-6
                  1 Peter 1:17-23

Our hope is anchored in
the <u>Presence</u> of Christ
the <u>Place</u> He has prepared
                  for us
the <u>Promise</u> that He will
come again and take
us with Him

Other Books by Anne Graham Lotz

The Vision of His Glory
God's Story
Just Give Me Jesus

Contents

Contents

A personal word for you
from my father …

On Tuesday, September 11, 2001, we all watched in horror as the twin towers of the New York World Trade Center erupted into raging fireballs after being struck by hijacked airliners. A tragedy that seemed to be as bad as it could be became dramatically worse when the buildings imploded. One hundred and ten stories of concrete, glass, and steel disintegrated into six stories of dust, soot, and twisted metal. The devastation was beyond belief.

Nevertheless, at ground zero, the search and rescue effort that gave way to a massive cleanup revealed that the foundations of the towers were still intact. And I was struck by the similarity between our lives and that of the towers. At times, we experience unexpected blows, not of hijacked airliners, but of such things as bankruptcy, death, disease, and marriage and family breakups. As devastating as these blows are, our foundation of faith in Jesus Christ is sure.

And that faith is a solid foundation that enables us to look forward with hope to our heavenly home.

Our age is one of terribly painful remembrances of the brevity and uncertainty of life. When all around us seems vulnerable to destruction and the constant threat of danger, we search for foundations that will hold. We seek answers to the questions that plague us: What happens to our loved ones who have been taken from us? Why are we here? Where are we going?

I am now an old man. More and more, I cling to the hope of the gospel message that I have preached all over the world. I have preached in times of relative peace and in times of great world crisis, to people in materialistic plenty and to people in great poverty, in countries of political stability and in regions torn by civil war and social strife—many different faces, circumstances, and histories, but all with the same foundational need to know God. Across the changes of a lifetime, I continue to return to the one sure foundation that has undergirded me since I first began: trust in a loving God Who never changes, Who invites us to draw close to Him in Jesus Christ.

This little book written by my daughter Anne sets forth the tremendous hope of God's promise that we may spend eternity with Him. Anne's words in these pages have already inspired and enlightened my wife, Ruth, and me, and I know they will you as well. I know of no one who has delved more deeply and prayerfully into God's Word or is more effective in conveying its truth than Anne is. Because of the Cross and the resurrection of Christ, we can look forward with confidence to an eternal home in Heaven. The words written here point us to the assurance that we have been given in the Word of God. You can look forward with me, with Anne, and with all of God's children to the joy of our Father's House.

May God bless you
with that hope today,

Billy Graham

... and from my Heavenly Father

∞

This book is developed from the following Biblical description of Heaven:

Then I saw a new heaven and a new earth, for the first heaven and the first earth had passed away, and there was no longer any sea. I saw the Holy City, the new Jerusalem, coming down out of heaven from God, prepared as a bride beautifully dressed for her husband. And I heard a loud voice from the throne saying, "Now the dwelling of God is with men, and he will live with them. They will be his people, and God himself will be with them and be their God. He will wipe every tear from their eyes. There will be no more death or mourning or crying or pain, for the old order of things has passed away."

He who was seated on the throne said, "I am making everything new!" Then he said, "Write this down, for these words are trustworthy and true."

He said to me: "It is done. I am the Alpha and the Omega, the Beginning and the End. To him who is thirsty I will give to drink without cost from the spring of the water of life. He who overcomes will inherit all this, and I will be his God and he will be my son. But the cowardly, the unbelieving, the vile, the murderers, the sexually immoral, those who practice magic arts, the idolaters and all liars—their place will be in the fiery lake of burning sulfur. This is the second death."

One of the seven angels who had the seven bowls full of the seven last plagues came and said to me, "Come, I will show you the bride, the wife of the Lamb." And he carried me away in the Spirit to a mountain great and high, and showed me the Holy City, Jerusalem, coming down out of heaven from God. It shone with the glory of God, and its brilliance was like that of a very precious jewel, like a jasper, clear as crystal. It had a great, high wall with twelve gates, and with twelve angels at the gates. On the gates were written the names of the twelve tribes of Israel. There were three gates on the east, three on the north, three on the south and three on the west. The wall of the city had twelve foundations, and on them were the names of the twelve apostles of the Lamb.

The angel who talked with me had a measuring rod of gold to measure the city, its gates and its walls. The city was laid out like a square, as long as it was wide. He measured the city with the rod and found it to be 12,000 stadia in length, and as wide and high as it is long. He measured its wall and it was 144 cubits thick, by man's measurement, which the angel was using. The wall was made of jasper, and the city of pure gold, as pure as glass. The foundations of the city walls were decorated with every kind of precious stone. The first foundation was jasper, the second sapphire, the third chalcedony, the fourth emerald, the fifth sardonyx, the sixth carnelian, the seventh chrysolite, the eighth beryl, the ninth topaz, the tenth chrysoprase, the eleventh jacinth, and the twelfth amethyst. The twelve gates were twelve pearls, each gate made of a single pearl. The great street of the city was of pure gold, like transparent glass.

I did not see a temple in the city, because the Lord God Almighty and the Lamb are its temple. The city does not need the sun or the moon to shine on it, for the glory of God gives it light, and the Lamb is its lamp. The nations will walk by its light, and the kings of the earth will bring their splendor into it.

On no day will its gates ever be shut, for there will be no night there. The glory and honor of the nations will be brought into it. Nothing impure will ever enter it, nor will anyone who does what is shameful or deceitful, but only those whose names are written in the Lamb's book of life.

—REVELATION 21

Even though I walk through
    the valley of the shadow of death,
I will fear no evil,
    for you are with me. . . .
And I will dwell in the house of the LORD forever.
                   —KING DAVID

In my Father's house are many rooms;
    if it were not so, I would have told you.
I am going there to prepare a place for you.
    And if I go and prepare a place for you,
I will come back and take you to be with me
    that you also may be where I am.
                   —JESUS CHRIST

Looking Forward
to
Heaven

≈

Knowing where you are going takes
the uncertainty out of getting there.

"*For I know the plans I have for you,*"
declares the Lord,
"*plans to prosper you and not to harm you,*
plans to give you hope and a future."
—*JEREMIAH 29:11*

Death is the great equalizer, isn't it? It doesn't matter if we have lived on this earth as:

> young or old
>> rich or poor
>>> famous or unknown
>>>> educated or ignorant
>>>>> powerful or weak
>>>>>> religious or atheistic
>>>>>>> athletic or crippled
>>>>>>>> healthy or sickly
>>>>>>>>> happy or depressed . . .
>>>>>>>>>> *we all die.*[1]

Still, death can come as an utterly unexpected surprise. More than five thousand men and women went to work at the World Trade Center in New York City on September 11, 2001, and began what they thought was just another routine day at the office. Many of them had likely gotten a cup of coffee, sat down at their desks, rolled up their sleeves, booted up their computers, and begun placing telephone calls. None of them had any indication that within the hour they would step into eternity. For them, death came as a thief in the night.

For others, death can come as a longed-for and welcomed relief. Within a three-week period, while I was in the midst of writing this book, I attended both the funeral of my husband's beloved brother, John Lotz, and the funeral of my father's associate T. W. Wilson, who was like a second father to me. John died as a result of a fast-growing, malignant brain tumor. "Uncle T" died from massive heart failure at the grand old age of eighty-two. For both John and Uncle T, death came as an angel of mercy.

Regardless of how or when it comes, *death does come* for each of us. And each of us wonders: *When will it come for my loved one? What will it be like for me?*

For the past thirteen years I have traveled all over the world in response to invitations to give out God's Word. There have been times, such as my first visit to India, when I have started out by climbing onto the plane with my stomach churning, my knees knocking, and my heart fibrillating—terrified because I was not sure where I was going, or who would meet me at the journey's end. But what a difference there has been in my attitude when I have had the opportunity for a second visit to that same place. I have left home with peace in my heart because I knew where I was going and who would meet me at the journey's end. In the same way, the prospect of death can fill you and me with terror and dread—unless we know where we are going. Knowing as much as we can about our final destination, and Who will meet us at the end of life's journey, takes the fear out of getting there.

Hope for Today

Picture an old man, living on a remote island. He is about ninety years of age, and he knows it will soon be his time to die. Like many elderly people today, he is isolated and lonely, cut off from family and friends at the very time of his life when he most needs them. He is frail and weak, facing the great unknown of eternity.

As incredible as it may seem, this man was one of the twelve original disciples of Jesus Christ. In fact, as one of the closest personal friends Jesus had, he was described as the "beloved disciple."

This was the apostle John, previously just a fisherman from Galilee. He and his brother James were the sons of Zebedee who earlier had been called the sons of thunder because they had such fiery tempers. But by the end of the first century, John was one of the most respected of all the disciples. And he paid a high price for his well-known and outspoken relationship with the One he believed to be the Messiah, the Son of God, Jesus of Nazareth.

Exiled to the island of Patmos in the midst of the Aegean Sea, the apostle John knew he would be facing death in the not-too-distant future. This was the very moment in time when God chose to give John a vision of the glory of Jesus Christ! This vision included a tantalizing glimpse into Heaven, where one day God Himself will live forever with His people. This glorious vision has been recorded in the final book of the Bible, Revelation, because John was commanded to write down what he saw. The vision was to be not only for his own personal comfort and encouragement but for all people down through the centuries who, when facing daily challenges, extraordinary circumstances, or even when plunging to certain death, could do so with courage and *with hope.*

Hope for Tomorrow

Are you facing the future with eyes wide shut, teeth clenched, body tensed, dreading your tomorrows and what they may hold? Do you feel as though you are standing on the brink of a deep, dark abyss of helplessness and despair, caught up in events involving yourself or your loved ones that are beyond your control? Regardless of what those events may be, no matter your mental or emotional or spiritual state, God's vision of the future can fill you with hope *right now . . .*

If you are elderly like John,

If you are facing death,

If you are lonely,

If you are isolated,

If you are cut off from friends and family,

If you are in emotional or mental or physical pain,

If you are facing the greatest unknown of your life,

If you are hopeless for any reason . . .

or

If you have a loved one who is elderly
    like John,
If you have a loved one who is facing death,
If you have a loved one who is lonely,
If you have a loved one who is isolated,
If you have a loved one who feels cut off from
    friends and family,
If you have a loved one in emotional, mental,
    or physical pain,
If you have a loved one who is facing the
    greatest unknown of his or her life,
If you have a loved one who is hopeless for any
    reason . . .

or

If you are spending time in a doctor's office
    or a hospital waiting room,
If Alzheimer's has you trapped in a long
    good-bye
    or if divorce has you trapped in a
    living death,
If you are going to a memorial service
    or you have been to a funeral,
If you have wept at a gravesite
    or shed tears in the night,

If you hear gunfire in the dark,
> or unknown footsteps on the walk,
If you are an unemployed worker facing
>> another day,
> or just a weary parent whose spouse
>> is away . . .

or
> If you are a doctor or nurse,
>> a caregiver or a funeral director,
> If you are an orphan or a widow,
>> a single parent or a minority,
> If you live in poverty or obscurity,
>> prison or pain,
> If you have been beaten or bound,
>> bruised or broken,
> If you are disabled or abused,
>> abandoned or accused,
> If you are lonely or confused,
>> wondering or worrying,
> If you are despised or rejected,
>> helpless or homeless . . .

. . . then it is *vitally* important for you to be prepared for that moment in time when you step into eternity!

As I contemplate the deaths of my loved ones—and yours . . .

As I contemplate our loss and the empty void in our hearts left by their absence . . . .

I am more grateful than ever that this life is not all there is!

Praise God! You and I can look *forward WITH HOPE!* because we have the blessed assurance of Heaven, My Father's House!

A Home
in
Heaven

❧

My Father's House is a home
prepared especially for you.

If I go and prepare a place for you,
*   I will come back and take you to be with me*
that you also may be where I am.
                              —JOHN 14:3

Home for me will always be my father's house—a log cabin nestled in the mountains of western North Carolina with a light in the window, a fire on the hearth, and a welcome embrace at the door. As I make the four-hour drive from my home to my father's house, my sense of expectancy heightens. Three hours into the journey I have the first glimpse of the mountains—a glimpse that never ceases to thrill me as I begin to climb in altitude through the foothills until I'm enfolded in the valleys and peaks of the Blue Ridge Mountains. My journey ends on a winding, one-lane road with hairpin curves and switchbacks that lead me to the door of my father's house.

The old log cabin, the flagstone steps, the nail-studded door, and the well-worn wooden plank floor of the entrance are not what have quickened my pulse or caused me to make the long drive. My motivation is simply the fact that this is *home!*

Home! What does that word mean to you? For me, "home" is synonymous with love, acceptance, comfort, and security. It is a place where my needs are met. It is a place where I can take my burdens and lay them down. It is a place not only where I can find answers but where my questions no longer seem to matter. When I feel discouraged under the pressure of responsibilities, or overwhelmed by the problems of daily life, or disappointed by shattered dreams, my heart turns toward that mountain cabin and those whom I love who live there. To go home is to be refreshed in my spirit and refocused in my thoughts and renewed in my strength and restored in my heart. How I love home!

The story is told of an old missionary named Samuel Morrison who, after twenty-five years in Africa, was returning home to the United States to die. As it so happened, he traveled on the same ocean liner that brought President Teddy Roosevelt back from a hunting expedition. When the great ship pulled into New York Harbor, the dock where it was to tie up was jammed with what looked like the entire population of New York City. Bands were playing, banners were waving, choirs of children were singing, multicolored balloons were floating in the air, flashbulbs were popping, and newsreel cameras were poised to record the return of the president.

Mr. Roosevelt stepped down the gangplank to thunderous cheers and applause, showered with confetti and ticker tape. If the crowd had not been restrained by ropes and police, he would have been mobbed!

At the same time, Samuel Morrison quietly walked off the boat. No one was there to greet him. He slipped alone through the crowd. Because of the crush of people there to welcome the president, he couldn't even find a cab. Inside his heart, he began to complain, *Lord, the president has been in Africa for three weeks, killing animals, and the whole world turns out to welcome him home. I've given twenty-five years of my life in Africa, serving You, and no one has greeted me or even knows I'm here.*

In the quietness of his heart, a gentle, loving voice whispered, *But My dear child, you are not home yet!*

While I praise God for placing me in an earthly home that so clearly reflects my heavenly home, I am aware even now, when I visit that old log cabin, that I am not really home yet because of Jesus' promise to

15

God's children: "In my Father's house are many rooms; if it were not so, I would have told you. I am going there to prepare a place for you. And if I go and prepare a place for you, I will come back and take you to be with me that you also may be where I am."[1]

Has your entire life been a series of struggles? Have you been . . .

More sick than well?

More defeated than successful?

More tired than rested?

More alone than accompanied?

More empty than satisfied?

More hungry than filled?

More sad than happy?

Do you feel defeated because after a lifetime of struggle, all you have to look forward to is death and a cold grave? Look up! The Bible teaches us that God is preparing a heavenly home that "no eye has seen, no ear has heard, no mind has conceived . . . for those who love him."[2]

Regardless of our circumstances or condition, we can look forward *with hope* as we glimpse Heaven, My Father's House, which is being prepared as an eternal home for God's people. For you and for me!

As a young girl, my vision of Heaven was framed by my mother's assurance that whatever was necessary for my eternal happiness would be there. So in my child's mind, that included ocean waves, mountain peaks, a favorite pet that had died, Sunday night Bible games with the family, sleepovers at my grandparents' house, Chinese food, and a smaller nose! Over the years, my requirements for eternal happiness have changed, but my dreams are still big.

What kind of home do you think is necessary for your eternal happiness?

Do you dream of a cottage by the sea?

or a chateau by the lake?

or a cabin in the woods?

or a penthouse in the city?

or a castle on the hill?

or a tent on the desert?

or a farm in the country?

or a palace in the garden?

Several years ago, the apostle John's words describing the tantalizing vision of Heaven that God gave to him on the island of Patmos came to my mind, sharpening the focus of my "dream home." I was in Agra, India, standing in front of a reflecting pool gazing at the spectacular beauty of the Taj Mahal when I remembered John's initial impression of Heaven: "Then I saw a new heaven and a new earth, for the first heaven and the first earth had passed away, and there was no longer any sea. I saw the Holy City, the new Jerusalem, coming down out of heaven from God, prepared as a bride beautifully dressed for her husband" (Rev. 21:1–2). Just as a bride lovingly prepares every detail of herself for her special bridegroom, God is preparing His heavenly home for you and me. This loving preparation is illustrated by the story of the Taj Mahal.

Prepared with Love

The Taj Mahal was prepared as a monument of love. It was built between 1632 and 1653 by Shah Jahan for his wife. Constructed of white marble, it glistens like a jewel on the bank of a wide river. It is framed by four minarets, each one placed at the corner of the red-sandstone platform on which the entire building sits, pointing like long, white fingers to the sky. The exterior of the white-marble structure is inlaid with black onyx in flowing script depicting quotes from the Koran. The interior, including walls and ceiling, is inlaid with semiprecious stones in floral designs that are symbols of the Islamic paradise.

How can one imagine the painstaking craftsmanship involved in completing a project that required over twenty thousand skilled workers and took more than twenty years to complete? How can one imagine the love that conceived such a project in the first place? Even more remarkable is the fact that the Taj Mahal was intentionally designed not as a palace or as a summer residence or even as an elaborate boathouse. The Taj Mahal is a tomb! It was built by the lavishly romantic and wealthy shah for his beloved wife, to whom he'd been married for only fourteen years when she was overtaken by the great equalizer—death. It's sad to think that although his wife was buried in this exquisite edifice, when the shah died, he was not allowed to be buried with her.

If one Indian ruler could prepare something as breathtakingly beautiful as the Taj Mahal as a *tomb* for his wife of just *fourteen years,* what must God be preparing as a *home* where He will *live forever and ever* with His people whom He loves?

Prepared in Detail

John saw My Father's House "prepared as a bride beautifully dressed for her husband" (Rev. 21:2). I doubt that there is anything more detailed than a wedding. I know! All three of my children got married within eight months of each other! My mind almost exploded with all the details! My daughters spent hours selecting just the right dress. Then they had to find the right headpiece to go with the dress—and whether it would be shoulder, fingertip, or chapel length. Next they searched for the right shoes to go with the dress, and after that they picked out just the right jewelry and the right hairdo and the right flowers and the right church and the right music and the right bridesmaids and the right bridesmaids' dresses and the right groomsmen and—praise God!—the right grooms! Then there was the selection of the place for the rehearsal dinners, the menus for the rehearsal dinners, the place for the receptions, the menus for the receptions, the bride and groom's cakes for the receptions, and the decorations for each event. And I haven't even mentioned the hours and hours of poring over the invitation list after deciding on the color, size, print, and style of the invitation itself! Preparing for a wedding can be a full-time job for months preceding the actual day. And all of this was just to prepare my brides for their husbands!

Of all these elaborate plans, no part of the preparation received more attention, thought, planning, and care than the appearance of the bride herself. And despite all the planning and attention to detail, both of my daughters at one point on the day of their weddings became hysterical over their appearance!

I remember the morning of my own wedding day. My mother brought me breakfast in bed, serving it on the new china and with the new silver I had been given as wedding gifts. After breakfast, I stayed in my bedclothes, resting and taking it easy, so I would be fresh for the marriage ceremony and the reception that would follow that evening. Several hours before I was to leave the house to go to the church, I began to get ready. I started with my makeup, carefully applying it in order to enhance any physical beauty I might have and hide the many flaws I did have! I worked on my hair, sweeping it up so it would stay under the veil yet be visible enough to frame my face. Finally my mother came to my room and helped me get into my wedding gown, fastening the dozens of small buttons up the back and adjusting the chapel-length veil. When I had done everything I knew to do to get myself ready, I just stood in front of the full-length mirror and gazed at the young woman enveloped in ivory silk and lace who was reflected in it. I was tense and eager as I wondered, after six and a half months of preparation, if I would be beautiful and desirable to my husband.

As elaborate as my preparations were as a bride seeking to be beautiful for my husband, they were feeble in comparison with the Lord God's preparations for His bride, beginning with the very first earthly home. The first book in the Bible, Genesis, gives us an unforgettable picture of the Lord God. After at least five "days" of intensely creative work, He "planted a garden in the east, in Eden; and there he put the man he had formed. And the LORD God made all kinds of trees grow out of the ground—trees that were pleasing to the eye."[3] In my mind's eye, I can see Him on His hands and knees, grubbing in the dirt, planting trees and flowers and shrubs and grass, watering and pruning and landscaping. God Himself was the first homemaker, preparing a place for His children, Adam and Eve, that would be pleasing to the eye. We can only imagine the joyful eagerness of the divine Gardener as He presented Adam with his lovingly prepared home that was not just adequate or sufficient to meet his needs but extravagant in its lush beauty and comfort.

But the preparations made for that first earthly home, like the preparations I made for my wedding, or my daughters made for their weddings, or like the shah made for his beloved wife's tomb, are nothing compared with the preparations being made for our heavenly home!

Prepared for You

Jesus promised, "I am going there to prepare a place for you."[4] That was approximately two thousand years ago! In Revelation 21:6 He proclaimed, "It is done. I am the Alpha and the Omega, the Beginning and the End." What God begins, He always completes. God's purpose that began at creation will one day be finished. His preparations will be completed, and My Father's House will be ready as a heavenly home for His loved ones.

When I know that my loved ones are coming home, especially my children who are now married and living away from me, I begin to prepare for them. My son, Jonathan, loves barbecued spareribs on the grill, a homemade apple pie, and time to play tennis with his dad. I prepare those things for him, so that when he walks through the door of the house he will know he was expected and welcome, because this is his home!

When my daughter Morrow comes home, I know that she loves a homemade chocolate pound cake, fresh flowers in her room, and time to look through home decorating catalogs. I prepare those things for her so that when she walks through the door, she will know she was expected and welcome, because this is her home!

Preparations for my daughter Rachel-Ruth are easy, because I know when she bursts through the door with her eyes sparkling, she's just glad to be home. Anything and everything suits her! But I know she likes lots of my time so she can sit and talk and talk and talk and talk. She also loves any kind of homemade rolls or biscuits or pastries—and especially chocolate fudge sauce on ice cream. And so I have those things waiting for her so that she also will know she was expected and welcome, because this is her home.

Considering how I prepare for my children when I know they are coming home, I love to think of the preparations God is making for my homecoming one day. He knows the colors I love, the scenery I enjoy, the things that make me happy, all the personal details that will let me know when I walk into My Father's House, I am expected and welcome, because He has prepared it for me! And in the same way, He is preparing a glorious homecoming for *you!*

The Home
of
Your Dreams

My Father's House is the home
you have always wanted.

"No eye has seen,
    no ear has heard,
    no mind has conceived
what God has prepared for those who love him,"—
but God has revealed it to us by his Spirit.
—1 CORINTHIANS 2:9–10

What is the home of your dreams? If you are . . .
an Eskimo living in an ice hut,
a Chinese living in a bamboo hut,
an African living in a mud hut,
a homeless person living in a newspaper hut,
a Bedouin living in a tent,
an Indian living in a teepee,
a royal living in a palace,
a tenant living in a project,
a slum dweller living in a shanty,
a president living in the White House,
a celebrity living in a penthouse,
a peasant living in a farmhouse,
a city dweller living in a rowhouse,
an orphan living in a foster house,
a criminal living in a prison house,

a soldier living in a guardhouse,

a beggar with no house at all . . .

it doesn't matter! We all have dreams of what home should be like.

Do you dream of a home you can never go back to, or a home you can never have?

Do you dream of a home with love and laughter and loyalty, with family and fun and freedom?

Do you dream of a home where you are accepted, encouraged, and challenged, forgiven, understood, and comforted?

Do you dream of a home that never was, or a home that never will be?

When did your home begin to unravel? Have you been blindsided by divorce or death or disease or depression or a thousand and one other difficulties that have turned your dreams into a nightmare?

There is hope! The home you've always wanted, the home you continue to long for with all your heart, is the home God is preparing for you! As John continued to gaze at the vision of the glory of Jesus Christ that God revealed to him, he must have stood in awed wonder of a "new heaven and a new earth" (Rev. 21:1). What he saw was confirmed by the words of the One Who was seated on the throne: "I am making everything new!" (Rev. 21:5). Imagine it: One day, in the dream home of My Father's House, *everything* will be brand-new!

No Separation

Following the terrorist attack on the World Trade Center in New York City and the Pentagon in Washington, D.C., our nation was gripped by the heartrending sight of thousands of individuals wandering the streets of lower Manhattan carrying pictures of their friends and family members who were missing. A fence lining one of the nearby parks became a memorial wall as hundreds of pictures were posted with detailed descriptions of what the missing loved ones were wearing, of where they worked, of when they were last seen—all in the hopes that those missing persons might be found. As the days dragged into weeks, it became apparent that there would be no more survivors. Just when our nation thought there were no more tears to weep, we wept uncontrollably as a seemingly endless stream of memorial services was begun and the separation between friends and loved ones was finalized. Each heart-wrenching, tearful good-bye made me long for My Father's House.

John reassured us that there will be no separation in Heaven when he said, "There was no longer any sea" (Rev. 21:1). Now, I love the sea. Every summer, I spend as much time there as I am able. I love to see the vast expanse of sky and water. I love to hear the waves crashing on the shore. I love to walk along the beach and feel the sand beneath my feet and the breeze blowing gently in my face. But the sea separates families and friends and entire continents from each other! In Heaven, there will be *nothing* that separates us from each other or from God. Ever!

No hard feelings or hurt feelings,
No misunderstandings or critical spirits,
No divorce or death,
No piles of rubble or prisons of debris,
No business trips or military call-ups,
No sickness or weakness,
No dangers or hardships,
No fires or famines or floods,
No wars or refugee camps or ethnic cleansing,
No racial or political or religious prejudice,
No religions or polls or denominations,
No class systems or economic sanctions or human slavery,
Nothing will ever separate us in My Father's House.

We will enjoy perfect health and harmony and unity and unbroken times together! There will not even be the natural separation between night and day because, "The city does not need the sun or the moon to shine on it, for the glory of God gives it light, and the Lamb is its lamp" (Rev. 21:23). Our heavenly home will glow and radiate with light from within—the light of God Himself and the glorious radiance of His presence.

I have been in some of the great cities of the world at night. I have looked out after sunset from Victoria Peak in Hong Kong during the Chinese New Year, and I have seen the lights transform the hills surrounding the harbor into a virtual fairyland. I have seen the lights of Capetown, South Africa, wrapped around Table Mountain at night forming a vast, jewel-studded skirt. I have seen Paris from Montmartre after dinner, stretched out for miles in an endless sea of light with the lighted outline of the Eiffel Tower beckoning like a finger to those who love beauty.

But even in those great cities with their millions of lights, there are still pockets of darkness. In our heavenly home, there will be no darkness at all. No one will ever stumble or be lost or unable to find his or her way. Jesus said, "I am the light of the world,"[1] and He also said *we* "are the light of the world."[2] The sole light in Heaven will be the light that comes directly from God through Jesus Christ, and that light will be reflected in the life of each one of His children! The entire city will be saturated with the glory and light of life, truth, righteousness, goodness, love, and peace. Your hope is sure! John said that he was instructed, "Write this down, for these words are trustworthy and true" (Rev. 21:5). You and I can look forward with confident hope—our heavenly home will be perfect!

No Scars

Because Heaven is perfect, there will be nothing to mar its beauty. My husband, Danny, and I bought the house we live in when it was twenty years old, and we have been living in it now for thirty years. Because it is about fifty years old, there are some stains I will never be able to remove, some cracks in the tile that can never be repaired, some wear and tear that gives the house a slightly frayed, worn-out look. It's just scarred by age. When I visit some of my friends in their brand-new homes, I look longingly at the fresh, unmarked woodwork and painted walls; the fresh, unstained carpet; the fresh, glistening tile and appliances; the fresh, unscratched windowpanes. It's all fresh! New! Unscarred, unsoiled, and unworn by age!

Planet earth is, at the very least, thousands of years old. Some think it may be millions or billions of years old. And it is showing signs of age. It is getting frayed and worn out. It is being polluted, gouged, stripped, burned, and poisoned, and much of the damage has been willfully and selfishly inflicted by man. But some of the scars are simply due to the wear and tear of age. It was not created to last forever!

In contrast, our heavenly home is going to be brand-new. Not just restored, but created fresh. John emphasized this again and again when he described "a *new* heaven and a *new* earth," and a "*new* Jerusalem," and once again the clear directive came from the One Who was seated on the throne, saying, "'I am making everything new!' Then He said, 'Write this down, for these words are trustworthy and true.'" God Himself was verifying that all His promises are true.

What scars of sin or stains of guilt do you bear in

your life? On your emotions? On your personality? On your relationships? On your memories? Like planet earth, do you feel abused and gouged and worn out and burned by other people? Does your life show the signs of wear and tear inflicted willfully and selfishly by those who have had authority over you? Have you ever longed to be able to start your life over again? Maybe you can even identify with the following testimony of a woman who spoke with me several years ago.

After presenting a message to a large convention, this woman came up to me and briefly told me her story. She described being raised in a family where her father and brothers repeatedly abused her sexually. She was so humiliated, angry, and bitter, she grew up to live a very immoral lifestyle. When she finally married and had a family, she abused her own children. One day she heard that God loved her and had sent His Son, Jesus Christ, to die in order to cleanse her of her sin. She responded by asking God to forgive and cleanse her for Jesus' sake, and she said she knew He had answered her prayer. "But," she softly cried, "I just can't seem to forget. What can I do about the memories?"

What could I say? There was nothing I could do except put my arms around her and tell her that one day there will be no more scars. God will wipe all tears away and erase all memories of such sin and abuse. *Everything*—including our heart, mind, emotions, psyche, and memories, past, present, and future—will be made new.

However, until then God does give us encouragement. His reassurance is illustrated by this true story that took place years ago in the Highlands of Scotland. A group of fishermen sat around a table in a small pub, telling their "fish stories." As one of the men flung out his arms to more vividly describe the fish that got away, he accidentally hit the tray of drinks that the young barmaid was bringing to the table. The tray and the drinks sailed through the air, crash-landing against the newly whitewashed wall. As the sound of smashed glass and splashing beer permeated the room, the pub became silent as all eyes turned to the ugly brown stain that was forming on the wall.

Before anyone could recover from the startling interruption, a guest who had been sitting quietly by himself in the corner jumped up, pulled a piece of charcoal from his pocket, and began to quickly sketch around the ugly brown stain. To the amazement of everyone present, right before their eyes the stain was transformed into a magnificent stag with antlers out-stretched, racing across a highland meadow. Then the guest signed his impromptu work of art. His name was Sir Edwin Landseer, Great Britain's foremost wildlife artist.

God transforms lives as Sir Landseer transformed the ugly mess on that pub wall. What ugly brown stain does your life bear? Like the woman at the convention, were you abused as a child? Have you abused some-one else's child? Or your own? Have you been raped? Have you been the victim of a violent crime? Have you had an abortion? Or performed one? Have you committed adultery? Or seduced someone else to do so? Is there a nasty addiction in your life to drugs? alcohol? pornography?

Regardless of what the stain is, submit it to God. You must be willing to turn away from any and all sin. Period. Then God excels in transforming ugly brown stains into beauty marks when we surrender them to Him. He will bring peace and freedom to you and glory to Himself. And when we get to Heaven there will be no more scars and no more suffering of any kind, including the kind that inflicted the wound that has scarred your life.

No Suffering

Heaven will not only *look* fresh and new, it will *feel* fresh and new! John gives us, not just a vision of Heaven's fresh beauty, but a "feel" of Heaven's serenity, which permeates the atmosphere because God is there: "And I heard a loud voice from the throne saying, 'Now the dwelling of God is with men, and he will live with them. They will be his people, and God himself will be with them and be their God. He will wipe every tear from their eyes. There will be no more death or mourning or crying or pain, for the old order of things has passed away'" (Rev. 21:3–4).

In what way are you suffering? Are you suffering . . .

Physically?

Emotionally?

Mentally?

Financially?

Materially?

Relationally?

Socially?

Spiritually?

One day, God Himself will take your face in His hands and gently wipe away your tears as He reassures

you there will be no more suffering in My Father's
House. No more . . .

        pain

           or hospitals

              or death

                 or funerals

                    or grief,

                       or walkers

                          or canes

                             or wheelchairs.

There will be no more . . .

        suicide bombers or fiery infernos,

      broken homes or broken hearts,

        broken lives or broken dreams.

There will be no more . . .

mental retardation or physical handicaps,

muscular dystrophy or multiple sclerosis,

  blindness or lameness,

    deafness or sickness.

There will be no more . . .

  Parkinson's disease or heart disease,

    diabetes or arthritis,

      cataracts or paralysis.

No more . . .
    cancer or strokes or AIDS.
No more . . .
    guns in schools
        or car bombs
            or terrorists
                or missiles
                    or air strikes.
No more war!

You can look forward with hope, because one day there will be no more separation, no more scars, and no more suffering in My Father's House. It's the home of your dreams!

A Home
That Is Safe

❦

My Father's House will keep you
and your loved ones from all harm and danger.

It had a great, high wall.
—*REVELATION 21:12*

On September 11, 2001, like millions of other Americans, I sat glued to my television set. The horrifying scenes of the jetliners crashing into the towers and the Pentagon, the erupting fireballs, and the imploding buildings that were played over and over again are indelibly frozen in my mind's eye.

I wonder how many parents were faced with teary, terrified children who returned home from school that Tuesday afternoon asking, "Mommy, Daddy, are we at war? Are we going to die? Will we be safe?" How did the parents answer? Did they speak the truth? Or did they just give hollow words of comfort because they had no answers?

While we cannot guarantee the safety of our children, or ourselves, or anyone else in this life, Jesus Christ does guarantee our safety in eternity. When you and I place our faith in Him as our Savior and yield our lives to Him as Lord, God promises that we "shall not perish but have eternal life."[1] And the "eternal life" will be lived with God and His family in My Father's House!

In Revelation 21 the apostle John describes the glimpse he was given into God's heavenly home. My Father's House is real! It is not:

an abstract idea

or a small child's fantasy

or an artist's concept of celestial beauty

or a musician's theme for a symphony

or a fearful person's imaginative escape from harm.

It is the only true home that will keep you and your loved ones happy, healthy, and safe—forever!

The angel who took John on a guided tour literally measured the dimensions of Heaven, emphasizing that it is indeed a literal, specific, physical, actual place: "The angel who talked with me had a measuring rod of gold to measure the city, its gates and its walls" (Rev. 21:15). The city he measured was exceedingly large!

Have you ever felt trapped in a small home?

or in a dormitory room?

or in a hospital bed?

or in a wheelchair?

or in an office cubicle?

or in a prison cell?

Then you can look forward to My Father's House!
Heaven is a very real place that will give you very real
freedom. You need never fear . . .

hijackers or bombers, terrorists or threats,

lawsuits or gunshots, bullets or bandits,

boundaries that stifle, roadblocks that stop,

limits that squelch, walls that strangle,

planes that crash, buildings that implode.

A Spacious Home

The angel who was giving the apostle John a guided
tour of My Father's House measured off a home that
was so spacious as to be almost beyond our compre-
hension. Although it remains to be seen if the meas-
urements John recorded can be taken literally, Dr.
Henry Morris, in his book *The Revelation Record,* has
calculated them mathematically.[2] They describe a
cube that is fifteen hundred miles square, which is as
large as the area from Canada to Mexico, and from
the Atlantic Ocean to the Rockies. It could easily
accommodate twenty billion residents, each having his

or her own private seventy-five-acre cube or room or mansion. This would still leave plenty of room for streets, parks, and public buildings. Heaven is a big place! "In my Father's house are many rooms"—room enough for anyone and everyone who chooses to be a member of God's family![3] So please feel free to invite your entire family—including in-laws and out-laws,

      every one of your friends,

    all of your neighbors,

   the total population of your city,

  your state, your nation—

everybody in the whole wide world!

Heaven is a great big place that is real! It is an actual place that can be felt and seen and measured! As we progressively destroy planet earth, it is exciting to contemplate that somewhere in the universe, at this very moment, our heavenly home is being prepared for us. As this world ends, a new world begins.

From time to time people have asked me, and I have wondered myself, what Heaven will be like. With no sea, will it be less enjoyable than earth and its mighty oceans? With no sunsets or sunrises or full moons or shooting stars, will it be less beautiful than the vast expanse that spreads over our earthly home?

I wonder . . . then I remember that Jesus knows exactly what brings me pleasure and joy! The Creator Who created all the earthly beauty we have grown to love . . .

> The majestic snowcapped peaks of the Alps,
> The rushing mountain streams,
> The brilliantly colored fall leaves,
> The carpets of wildflowers,
> The glistening fin of a fish as it leaps
>   out of a sparkling sea,
> The graceful gliding of a swan across the lake,
> The lilting notes of a canary's song,
> The whir of a hummingbird's wings,
> The shimmer of the dew on the grass
>   in early morning . . .

This is the *same* Creator Who has prepared our heavenly home for us! If God could make the heavens and earth as beautiful as we think they are today—which includes thousands of years of wear and tear, corruption and pollution, sin and selfishness—can you imagine what the new Heaven and the new earth will look like? It will be much more glorious than any eyes have seen, any ears have heard, or any minds have ever conceived![4] And John saw it!

A Secure Home

John gazed on "a great, high wall . . . made of jasper" that surrounds our future home (Rev. 21:12, 18). The wall is described as being over two hundred feet thick and made of jasper, a gemstone resembling a diamond! Can you imagine the beauty of two-hundred-foot-thick walls made of "diamonds" that reflect the light of God? Can you imagine the safety of those who live inside walls that are two hundred feet thick?! The walls are so strong that God's loved ones will be eternally secure.

Have you ever been the victim of a violent crime? A drive-by shooting? Rape? Robbery? Mugging? Has one of your children ever been the victim of a violent crime or perhaps been involved in a tragic car accident?

Several years ago my husband and I were cruising the Aegean Sea on a beautiful ship as the guests of friends when I received word that the captain on the bridge wished to speak with me. When I went up, he told me I had an incoming phone call on the ship's radio. When I answered and identified myself, a young man's voice came over the receiver. He was the son of a dear friend who had been a tennis buddy and member of my Bible class. He told me that his mother and father had been walking in the cool of the evening down their little country lane when a car that was passing by suddenly swerved, taking the life of his mother. He was calling to ask me to speak at her funeral. I agreed.

Shortly after arriving home, I stood in front of a packed church overflowing with shocked, grieving friends and family members. As simply as I could, I told them about My Father's House, where my friend had gone to live forever. And I took comfort in knowing she was safely inside those two-hundred-foot-thick walls!

When my three children were growing up, I did all I knew to do to ensure their safety. Childproof caps on medicines, chemicals up out of reach, seat belts securely fastened, hands tightly held as we walked, stern warnings about fire and electrical outlets, all were part of the normal, daily routine. When they grew up they went off to college, then to other homes and cities where I could not supervise. There was no way of tracking moment by moment what they were involved in or who they were involved with. But I had a deep peace because all of my children, when they were young, had placed their faith in Jesus Christ as their own Savior. I knew they had been born again into the family of God and therefore, My Father's House is also their own. Regardless of what happened here in this life, I knew they were eternally secure.

What have you done to ensure that your children will be safe in eternity? Don't leave the issue of your child's safety up to the church, or a school, or a "professional" religious leader. It's your responsibility and privilege to tell your children about God, about their own sin, about their need to claim Jesus Christ as their Savior so their sins will be washed away, about their Father's House and how to get there. If for any reason you no longer have the opportunity to ensure their "safety," then just pray, trusting God for the safety He will one day provide for you and asking Him to work on behalf of your children.

When I read . . .

> of overcrowded slums,
> of disintegrating shantytowns,
> of sweatshops,
> of slave labor,
> of drive-by shootings,

of drug addictions,
of terrorist attacks,
of the tremors of earthquakes,
of incurable diseases,
of untimely deaths,
of mysterious disappearances,
of missile strikes,
of gang rapes,
of violent robberies,
of financial failures,
of business bankruptcies,
of stock market fluctuations,
of military invasions,
of racial hatred,
of social injustice,
of national corruption,
of political oppression,
of weapons of mass destruction,
of germ warfare,
I praise God for My Father's House, which is safe and
secure—forever!

A Home
You Can Never Lose

✦

My Father's House is built to last.

Therefore,
since we are receiving a kingdom that cannot be shaken,
let us be thankful,
and so worship God acceptably with reverence and awe.
—HEBREWS 12:28

Nothing is more discouraging than building a new house or remodeling an old one, only to find, a year after the project is finished, that the roof leaks, the floors creak, the plumbing breaks, the windows stick, and it just generally does not hold up to the wear and tear of day-to-day living. How many times do we hear some frustrated homeowner comment wistfully, "They just don't build houses like they used to"? He or she knows that many older homes were built to last while modern construction can be less enduring.

The twin towers of the World Trade Center in New York City were built in the 1960s and 1970s, and they were built to last. Skilled architects and rugged construction workers toiled seven years to complete the two buildings. The towers were constructed with steel beams running every thirty-six inches from the basements of the buildings to the tops of the 110 floors. They were built to withstand the impact of one of the largest airplanes of that day. But on September 11, 2001, following the fiery impact of modern jetliners loaded to capacity with jet fuel, both towers imploded in billowing clouds of dust and ashes and twisted metal. The twin towers, built to last for generations, had not even lasted for one.

In 1912, the largest and most luxurious ship ever built at that time, the RMS *Titanic,* set sail from England on its maiden cruise, bound for America. The opulently appointed vessel was 852 feet long and boasted sixteen watertight compartments to keep its passengers safely afloat no matter what hazards befell the ship at sea. The *Titanic* was said to be the safest ship ever built. And since it was thought to be unsinkable, lifeboats seemed like a frivolous waste of space. The great ship carried only half the number needed to accommodate its twenty-two hundred passengers and crew. Perhaps wondering about that shortage as the great ship set sail, one of the passengers purportedly asked a deckhand, "Is the *Titanic* really unsinkable?"

"God Himself couldn't sink the *Titanic!*" replied the cocky seaman.

But then, just before midnight on a clear, moonless

night in the North Atlantic, the *Titanic* struck an iceberg and sank less than three hours later, carrying nearly fifteen hundred souls into eternity. The great, "unsinkable" ship, built to last for several lifetimes, had sunk on its first voyage.

Heaven Is Permanently Yours

My Father's House is a home built to last, not just for a lifetime, but forever! As John continued to gaze on the spectacular vision God gave him, he described Heaven as a city with foundations: "The wall of the city had twelve foundations, and on them were the names of the twelve apostles of the Lamb. . . . The foundations of the city walls were decorated with every kind of precious stone" (Rev. 21:14, 19). The walls of Heaven are actually built on twelve foundations, each one decorated with a different gem. In addition to the spectacular beauty that is implied, we can be assured that Heaven is eternal and unshakable. It's permanent!

Every day the front pages of our newspapers carry stories of suicide-bombing attacks, of family massacres, of political intrigue and national upheavals, of stock market fluctuations, of environmental disasters—and the accounts continue on the newspapers' second pages. And the third pages. Our world is a very unstable place. We can never be certain of the future for ourselves or for the next generation. The fear and apprehension of what's around the corner of our lives can be paralyzing. But when we get to Heaven, we will be certain and sure of absolute, total, infinite stability.

Heaven Is Personally Yours

Each of Heaven's twelve foundations is also engraved with the name of one of "the twelve apostles of the Lamb" (Rev. 21:14), who were responsible for making Jesus Christ known to the world. I wonder what John thought as he gazed at the heavenly city and saw his own name engraved on one of the foundations. What a thrill it must have been when he realized all of his work for God and his witness for Jesus Christ, for which he had been beaten, imprisoned, and now exiled, had been stored up for him in Heaven as a glorious treasure![1] His life's work was all worth it because it had eternal value. His hope was found in Heaven. Personally!

And I wonder, how will Abraham feel when he sees the city for the first time? About four thousand years ago, Abraham left Ur of the Chaldees, looking for "the city with foundations, whose architect and builder is God."[2] As he followed God in a life of faith, he lived in a tent that he constantly moved from place to place. He never settled down. He never was allowed to put down roots or have any kind of permanent residence. He knew he was just an alien and a stranger on earth—just a pilgrim passing through to a great eternal city with foundations.[3]

Can you imagine the thrill that will be Abraham's when he bursts through the gates of My Father's House, shouting, "I've found it! I've finally found it! I've found what I was looking for! I've found what I have been hoping for! All the days and nights of wandering and living in tents were worth it. All of God's promises are true!" All of Abraham's goals and hopes and dreams—those things that were the driving motivational forces in his life—had been focused on his eternal home, and he will not be disappointed!

My husband has played basketball all of his life. He grew up playing in the streets of New York City, in backyard lots, on playground courts, and even in an old barn his father had converted for that purpose. One of his childhood dreams was realized when he was given a four-year scholarship to play at a major university. The second year he played at the university, his team went undefeated for thirty-two straight games. They not only won the NCAA national championship, but their season set an all-time record that still stands. It was the accomplishment of a lifelong goal that had consumed hours and hours of time, effort, and energy. Danny describes the experience of winning that final game for the national championship—in triple overtime!—as a thrill he had never experienced before or since. But within a few short hours, the thrill was gone, an emptiness set in, and he wondered, *Is that all there is?* A dust-collecting plaque, a few newspaper clippings that have grown yellow, and memories that have faded with time are all that are left of the thrill that was the dream and achievement of a lifetime.

When the game of life is over and we step into eternity, I wonder how many people will have that same empty feeling of, *Is that all there is? Is that all there is to my life's work and dreams and achievements?*

The hard-earned degrees,
   the fought-for position,
      the worldwide reputation,
        the accumulated wealth,
          the bulging résumé,
            the designer homes,
              the fashionable clothes,
              the collector's art,
              the priceless jewels,
                the exotic trips,
                  the gourmet meals,
                    the toned physique,
one day will disintegrate into eternal nothingness. Will your life have been wasted because it had no real eternal significance? Will you shake your head as you look back on the ashes of your wasted life and groan, "Is that all there is to show for a lifetime of living and working?"

Or, one day, like Abraham, as you enter My Father's House, will you be shouting, "This is it! I found it! I finally found it! Everything I dreamed of and sought after is here! All the sacrifice I made on earth has been compensated a hundred times over in Heaven! It was all worth it! I found all I hoped for and so much more—in My Father's House! Forever!"

A Home
of
Lasting Value

My Father's House is a good investment.

Store up for yourselves treasures in heaven,
where moth and rust do not destroy,
and where thieves do not break in and steal.
—Matthew 6:20

Gold is one of our most precious commodities. We hoard gold, we wear gold, we invest in gold, we work hard for more gold—we love gold! We sacrifice our families, our friends, our reputations, our health—all so that we can increase our supply of earthly treasures. We want to buy more things . . .

so we can dust more things

so we can break more things

so we can sell more things

so we can get more things

so we can show off more things

so we can rearrange more things

—none of which will last!

Living Treasures

The city and streets within My Father's House are spectacular: "The wall was made of jasper, and the city of pure gold. . . . The great street of the city was of pure gold" (Rev. 21:18, 21). Think of it! Layers and layers of it, tons and tons of it, miles and miles of it stretching out in all directions beneath our feet. If the apostle John hasn't already conveyed to us that My Father's House is spectacular, his description of the streets surely does. But I wonder if there is a subtle message to us contained in his description—a message that my wise mother, with her characteristic humor, pointed out to me when she dryly exclaimed that you can tell what God thinks of gold because He paves the streets of heaven with it! Gold is really just heavenly asphalt! In other words, there are many things down here on earth that we give a top priority to, which in eternity will be inconsequential and insignificant.

It's sobering to contemplate how much time, effort, sacrifice, compromise, and attention we give to acquiring and increasing our supply of something that is totally insignificant in eternity. What are *your* priorities? As you live them out, will they have eternal value and significance? Jesus commanded His disciples not to lay up treasures on earth where moth and rust corrupt and where thieves break in and steal, but to lay up treasures in Heaven.[1] I wonder what treasures we will have in Heaven as evidence of our work and witness on earth—if any?

It has been said that no one has ever seen a U-Haul behind a hearse! There is nothing we can take to Heaven with us—*or is there . . . ?*

- When my children were young I struggled morning after morning to get their attention for daily Bible reading and prayer. Week after week I dragged them, often with untied shoes and uncombed hair, to Sunday school and church. Evening after evening I read Bible stories to them and tried to explain the simplest truths of God's Word. Eventually, my children responded by claiming Jesus personally as their own Savior. Praise God! *Praise God!* My children will join me in My Father's House! My investment in their lives will result in a glorious "payoff" in Heaven!

- The missionary who spoke was dressed so unfashionably. He spoke haltingly and fidgeted nervously in front of the congregation of well-dressed, relatively affluent and spoiled American church members. But the report that he gave began to describe vividly what God was doing in a remote, almost forgotten part of the world. When the collection plate was passed, I gave all the money I had with me at the time. After a few more weeks of furlough, the missionary returned to his field of service. He sends me newsletters of his activities. A picture in his newsletter showed him baptizing a small group of new believers in a dirty river. As I contemplated the eternal life-change Jesus had made in the lives of those in the picture, I experienced a thrill. Praise God! I am going to take the return on my investment in that missionary's ministry to My Father's House!

• The historic church was centrally located in one of the world's major capitals. The sanctuary had been packed and the overflow rooms crammed to capacity by people who were eager to hear a word from the Lord. I had just delivered the evening message when she stood in front of me. She was pencil-thin, young, with a somewhat startled expression on her face. With the help of another woman, she haltingly told me that she had just come to the city from Beijing, China. Her curiosity about Christianity had drawn her into the crowded church service where she had encountered Jesus Christ and prayed to receive Him as her Savior. I asked her if she had any questions. Then I put my arms around her and praised God. I knew that one day I would join this trembling young girl in My Father's House! In essence, I will take her with me to Heaven!

• My daughter ran into my house, clutching an e-mail she had just received in our ministry office. It was from a man on the West Coast who had watched as I was interviewed on national television, and as a result had purchased my book *Just Give Me Jesus*. The e-mail described his desperate search for meaning—something to fill the emptiness in his life that constantly gnawed at him in spite of his busy schedule and multitude of friends. His search had ended as he read the book and focused on Jesus. He committed his life to Jesus and exclaimed that he would never be the same! The tears in my daughter's eyes were mirrored by my own, and I knew I would take this young man with me to My Father's House!

• The package was delivered to me at a conference center where I was leading a three-day seminar. When I opened it, I found a tattered, stained paperback copy of my book *God's Story*. As I examined it, I saw that it was underlined, dog-eared, and weathered, and had obviously been read over and over again. Inside was a letter from a woman who wrote that she had seen a homeless man begging at the door of a McDonald's restaurant. When she inquired if she could buy him a meal, he had refused but asked her if she would mail a book to the author. Then he handed her *God's Story*. She dutifully mailed it to my father's organization, which then forwarded it to the conference center where it was delivered to me.

When I opened the flyleaf, I found scrawled across it bits and pieces of the homeless man's testimony. He was a Vietnam vet. An alcoholic. Hardened. Embittered. One of the millions of men and women who wander the streets of our cities. One day as he sat begging, someone passing by handed him, not money, but this paperback book. He wrote that he had been reading it for days and weeks and months. Through its pages, he had found the love of God. His bitterness had been removed, his hardness had been softened, and he had committed his life to Jesus Christ. The book is now on my shelf as a constant reminder to pray for this homeless man whom one day I will take to My Father's House.

When Jesus said to lay up for ourselves treasures in Heaven, He was speaking of those whom we would either directly or indirectly lead to salvation through faith in Him. As I reflect on the untold hours of studying a passage of Scripture until it "breaks open" and I can make sense of how to relate it to my life and to the lives of others; as I reflect on the nights of agony and tears as I wrestle in prayer for those to whom I am sent; as I reflect on the miles and miles of travel that put huge distances between myself and my family; as I reflect on the almost unbearable pressures of being on a public platform, scrutinized by the sympathetic, the curious, and the critical; as I reflect on the stomach-churning fear of stepping out of my comfort zone in order to take a step of faith in obedience to God's command . . .

As I contemplate all the sacrifices required in order to live a life that is totally focused on Jesus Christ and His eternal kingdom, the joy seeps out of my heart onto my face in a smile of deep satisfaction. While my entrance into Heaven may not be as abundant as someone else's and my hoard of heavenly treasures may be smaller than yours, I know that at least I will not be empty-handed nor will I have to face the ashes of a wasted life when I get to My Father's House.[2] I will have some things—some-ones—to take with me!

Lasting Treasures

When Jesus said to lay up for ourselves treasures in Heaven, He was speaking not only of those we would lead to faith in Him but also of our own character that increasingly is conformed by God's Spirit into His own image. This is another subtle message that is conveyed by the streets of My Father's House.

The streets of our heavenly home are not only

made of pure gold but, amazingly and almost incomprehensively, they are also described as being as transparent as glass: "The great street of the city was of pure gold, like transparent glass" (Rev. 21:21). Surely gold that is polished until it looks like transparent glass would function as a mirror. Then everything that moves or walks along those streets would be reflected throughout our home.

The Bible tells us that when we get to Heaven all of our sins and flaws will fall away, and we will be like Jesus.[3] With our unique personalities and characteristics, every single one of us is going to perfectly reflect the character of Christ. And as we walk on streets that reflect like mirrors, every step we take and every move we make is going to bring glory to Him.

Do you ever get frustrated with the habits of sin in your life? I do! Even though I have been to the Cross and received forgiveness for all my sin, I still sin. I don't want to. I try not to. I hate sin! But I still sin. The reality of sin is the single most discouraging, defeating, depressing fact in my life. But I can look forward with hope. Because one day, when I get to My Father's House, all of my sin . . .

my sinful tendencies
my sinful thoughts
my sinful actions
my sinful attitudes
my sinful habits
my sinful words
my sinful feelings . . .

all my sins are going to fall away like a stinking garment that finally drops off and is discarded. What will be left at that point will be the character of Christ that has developed in me during my life on earth.[4]

When I obeyed Him in the midst of suffering . . .
When I trusted Him with unanswered prayer . . .
When I loved Him without having seen Him . . .
When I believed in Him even though all
        evidence was contrary to His Word . . .
When I focused on Him in the darkness of
        depression and discouragement . . .
When I hoped in Him alone to bring
        me through . . .
His character was being formed in me.[5]

When I chose to be patient instead of frustrated . . .
When I chose to love instead of hate . . .

When I chose to hold my tongue instead of lash
    out in anger . . .
When I chose to gently instruct instead of
    harshly correct . . .
When I chose to be gracious instead of rude . . .
When I chose to be kind instead of mean . . .
When I chose to be unselfish instead of selfish . . .
When I chose to give up my rights instead
    of insisting on them . . .
When I chose to tell the truth instead of lie . . .
His character was being formed in me.[6]

When I chose to submit to the pain . . .
When I chose to accept the pressure . . .
When I chose to bear the burden . . .
When I chose, every day, to deny myself and take
    up the cross of His will for my life that
    includes suffering . . .
When I chose to follow Him and not the crowd . . .
When I chose to live by His Word, not by the
    opinions of others . . .
His character was being formed in me.[7]

And it's His character, revealed in and through me,
that will be reflected throughout My Father's House!

As we totally yield our lives to the control of God's Spirit within us, He uses:

the responsibilities and relationships and ridicule,

the opportunities and obstacles and obligations,

the pressures and pain and problems,

the success and sickness and solitude . . .

He uses *all things* to work for our ultimate good, which is increasing, progressive, glorious conformity to the image of Jesus Christ![8]

As you and I lay up for ourselves living, lasting treasures in Heaven, we come to the awesome conclusion that we ourselves are *His* treasure! When God the Father looked throughout the universe for something to give His only Son in reward for what He had accomplished on earth, the Father handpicked you! You are the Father's priceless gift of love to the Son![9] And one day He will display His priceless treasures before the universe—in My Father's House!

A Home
That's Paid For

My Father Himself
has paid off the House.

For God so loved the world
    that he gave his one and only Son,
that whoever believes in him
    shall not perish
but have eternal life.
                                    —JOHN 3:16

Before we were married, Danny bought a small home for us, sight unseen to me. When we returned from our honeymoon, he took me straight to this little four-room house, where we lived for the next five years. In order to purchase the house, he had taken out a mortgage so that our monthly payments were stretched out over thirty years. If we had taken the full thirty years to pay off the mortgage, we would have ended up paying triple the purchase price of the home because the payments included interest to the bank where he had borrowed the money. It was a difficult prospect to face, but we were strapped and we could not manage larger monthly payments. He held down three jobs and I worked part-time just to meet those monthly payments. We dreamed of one day having our house paid for.

After five years, we sold the house for more than we had paid for it, which enabled us to have the money for the down payment on our next home. The new house was more expensive than the previous one, with larger monthly payments. With children soon arriving on the scene, I could not work even part-time outside of the home, so we struggled to get by on Danny's income. Even though his dental practice had begun to flourish, we still lived hand-to-mouth, with the monthly payments once again determining the rest of our cash flow. And we kept dreaming of having our house paid for.

But that dream faded as the reality of life set in. All three of our children were in college at the same time. All three had weddings within the same year. And so Danny and I settled in to a lifetime of making monthly payments on a home that never seemed any closer to being paid for than when we began. Many people still dream of having their houses paid for . . .

My beloved father-in-law was a street-corner preacher in New York City. The small churches he pastored on the weekends were not able to support him and his family sufficiently, so he also worked full-time for the New York Telephone Company. He paid forty-eight hundred dollars for the home on

Long Island where my husband went to junior and senior high school. When my father-in-law died approximately thirty-five years after the initial purchase of the home, he owed more than *one hundred thousand dollars* on it! He had mortgaged and remortgaged and remortgaged his home in order to meet the needs of his family as well as to satisfy his insatiable appetite for theological books. Ever-increasing monthly payments were a built-in part of his life. For Danny's father, a home that was paid for was, at best, a very remote dream!

The payment for My Father's House began before time when God decided to bring you and me into existence.[1] In the beginning of human history, God created you and me to live with Him forever. Eden was the garden paradise that He personally handcrafted as a home in which we would live with Him. But, represented by Adam and Eve, the human race rebelled against the Creator's plan, and consequently, paradise was lost.

Still, the Creator did not forget or abandon those whom He had created for Himself. At a predetermined time, He sent His own Son to die on the Cross in order to take away our sin, bring us back into a right relationship with Himself, and open once again the gates to His heavenly home. Our home in Heaven has been paid for, once and for all! We won't have to worry about . . .

good works

or religiosity

or church attendance

or rituals

or traditions . . .

My Father's House has been bought and paid for in full with the blood of His own dear Son!

Are you struggling with the monthly payments on your house? Or the monthly rent on an apartment? Do you share the dream of one day living in a place that's paid for? Then that's one more reason you can look forward with hope to Heaven!

The payment for our heavenly home is symbolized by perhaps the single most spectacular characteristic that John describes—the gates. Incredibly, "the twelve gates were twelve pearls, each gate made of a single pearl" (Rev. 21:21). Can you imagine how large those pearls would have to be, to be set in walls that are two hundred feet thick?

Pearls are formed when a small grain of sand becomes

embedded in an oyster, irritating it. To soften the irritation, the oyster coats the grain of sand with a smooth layer of what is called mother of pearl. As long as the oyster can feel the irritation, it continues to coat the sand with layers of pearl. What kind of irritation would have been necessary to form the pearls that make up the gates to our heavenly city when they are so large they can fit into a wall that is *two hundred feet thick?!* It must have been more than just irritation. It must have been horrendous, severe suffering!

I wonder . . . are the pearls a reminder, every time you and I enter My Father's House, that we enter only because of the intense suffering of God's Son? Do those pearly gates reflect the Cross of Jesus Christ? Will they be a continual reminder to us of what it cost Him personally to throw open the gates of that city and welcome us home? Just imagine: As we enter our heavenly home through portals of pearl, we will be enveloped by symbols of His sacrificial love for us.

Do you know someone who says the Cross is unnecessary? That there are other ways to God besides claiming the death of Jesus Christ for sin?

That . . .

   if you just do more good works than bad works,

     if you go to church at least twice a year,

       if you are sincere in whatever religion you choose,

        if you are good,

          if you are moral,

then God will "owe" you a heavenly home? That there are human ways to make the "house payments"?

Or could it be that the very gates through which anyone enters Heaven will say, by their very presence, *there is no other way to enter except through the death— the Cross—of Jesus Christ!* Our heavenly home is debt-free, bought and paid for by the very blood of God's only Son! Finally, ultimately, eternally, our dream of living in a home that is paid for will be realized, because Jesus has paid it all!

A Home
Filled with Family

In My Father's House,
we will live with Him forever.

Now the dwelling of God is with men,
    and he will live with them.
They will be his people,
    and God himself will be with them
    and be their God.

—REVELATION 21:3

On a recent trip to London, I made the time to buy a ticket and tour Buckingham Palace, the home of the queen of England and her family. I passed through one spectacular room after another. I saw . . .

hand-painted ceilings,
magnificent, museum-quality tapestries,
masterpieces of art,
priceless porcelains,
gilded furniture,
crystal chandeliers,

and other treasures too numerous and awesome to describe. But nowhere did I see a child's toy, or a family photograph, or an open magazine, or a jacket casually thrown over a chair, or a table set for two, or even a coffee cup sitting on a side table. As I expected, Buckingham Palace is a magnificent showplace, but it's hard to think of it as a *home*.

While My Father's House is the most beautiful

place ever imagined, it's not a museum or a mere showplace—it is definitely a home! It's the home of the Lord God Almighty and the Lamb. John said, "I did not see a temple in the city, because the Lord God Almighty and the Lamb are its temple" (Rev. 21:22).

The Father Will Be There

The Greek word for "temple" is, in this case, the same word used for the "Most Holy Place," which was the inner sanctuary of the ancient Israelites' tabernacle, and later the temple. It was the place where God was said to dwell. The high priest could only enter once a year to sprinkle the sacrificed animals' blood on the mercy seat in order to make atonement for the sin of God's people.[1] The Book of Hebrews teaches us that today "we have confidence to enter the Most Holy Place by the blood of Jesus, by a new and living way opened for us through the curtain, that is, his body."[2] In other words, through the death and broken body of Jesus Christ on the Cross, you and I have been given access to the presence of God when we approach Him by faith in prayer.

In our heavenly home, we will not just have

occasional access to the presence of God; we will *live* in His presence! Every moment! Every day! Every week and month and year! For all eternity!

Before I realized this truth, I was troubled by a nagging worry that when we get to Heaven, you would live over there, and I would live over here, and God would live out there, and maybe one day He would come to visit me in my mansion, then leave and go visit you in yours. In other words, I thought there would be times when I would not be in His actual, visible presence. I had almost a sense of panic in that my whole life has been yielded to the presence of the Holy Spirit, and my entire aim is to be filled with Him in every nook and cranny of my heart, mind, soul, and body. But when I arrived in Heaven, would I have to trade His constant, invisible, indwelling presence for the occasional joy and blessing of the visible presence of Jesus? As I have grown to depend on Him so completely, and to enjoy Him so personally, and to count on Him so faithfully, and to love Him so passionately, the thought of being without Him for even a moment was truly frightening. Heaven became something to dread and avoid and postpone as long as I could.

How foolish my thoughts and fears were! As I meditated on this passage, I came to realize that when John said, "The Lord God Almighty and the Lamb are its temple," he was describing our entire heavenly home as the Most Holy Place. There will be *no place* in Heaven where God is not physically, actually present! Because He is omnipresent, He will live fully and completely with me every moment, as though I were the only resident of Heaven! And He will live every moment fully and completely with you as though you were the only resident of Heaven! What a wonderful place Heaven will be!

Our Loved Ones Will Be There

Not only will we live with Him, but we will live with our loved ones who have died trusting Jesus Christ as their Savior. I have family and friends waiting for me . . .

Lao Niang and Lao E, my maternal grandparents,
Mother and Daddy Graham, my paternal
    grandparents,
Gramma and Grampa, my mother- and
    father-in-law,

Sam and John, my brothers-in-law,
Two unborn babies,
Uncle Clayton and Uncle Sam,
Miss A. Wetherell Johnson, my beloved teacher
    and mentor,
Pearl Hamilton, my mentor and friend,
Kip Jordon, my first publisher,
Jamie and Nancy and Uncle T and Ted . . .

. . . and the list keeps growing every day. Who do you know who trusted Jesus alone as their Savior and Lord, someone who has died and gone before you to My Father's House? While you and I may grieve, we don't grieve as those who have no hope.[3] We know that one day we will live with them—the Lord and the Lamb and *our loved ones*—forever and ever![4] Now, that's a comforting hope![5]

As wonderful as my loved ones are and as much as I miss them, they were not perfect! And if your loved ones are like mine, your relationship with them on earth has not been perfect either. To think of living forever in the same home with my brother Franklin would give one pause![6] But when we get to Heaven, the joy of seeing our loved ones once again is immeasurably increased when we realize

that *all* of us will indeed be perfect![7] There will be
no more . . .

    disagreements or cross words,
      hurt feelings or misunderstandings,
        neglect or busyness,
          interruptions or rivalry,
        jealousy or pride,
         selfishness or sin
          of any kind!

There will be nothing at all to mar our full enjoyment
of being with our loved ones forever and ever!

On the other hand, do you know someone who
has died, but you are unsure he or she ever claimed
Jesus as Savior and Lord? Then, like Abraham, would
you trust the Judge of all the earth to do right?[8] Who
knows but that your loved one, like the thief on the
cross, trusted Jesus at the last moment?[9]

Several survivors of the attack on the World Trade
Center in New York City shared publicly that when
they were trapped in a flaming elevator or smoke-
filled stairwell and were convinced they were going
to die, they began praying, confessing their sins and
asking God to forgive them. If these survivors reacted
by crying out to God for mercy, I wonder how many

more people—not just victims at the World Trade Center but those who have died throughout generations—perhaps trusted in Christ at the last moment.

However, to prevent your friends and loved ones from having this same uncertainty when you die, make sure they know today that you trust Jesus as your Savior and Heaven is your Father's House.

The Household Servants Will Be There

Not only will the Lord God, the Lamb, and His loved ones live in the heavenly city, but the leaders of the nations of the earth will also come in and out of it. John described his view of the procession: "The nations will walk by its light, and the kings of the earth will bring their splendor into it. On no day will its gates ever be shut, for there will be no night there. The glory and honor of the nations will be brought into it" (Rev. 21:24–26).

Who are these leaders of the nations of the earth? Since we are told the only ones who enter the heavenly city are those whose names are written in the Lamb's book of life, the leaders and kings who come and go must be redeemed humanity—those who have deliberately, consciously placed their faith in Jesus Christ alone as Savior and Lord. That means me! And it includes you! Because apparently, in some way we don't fully understand, God's children will be given positions of leadership and responsibility in the new earth so that we might uniquely serve Christ for all eternity. The highest positions of authority in the universe will actually be positions as Household servants. No matter where our service takes us or what our service is, it will ultimately be for the glory of Christ.

My former brother-in-law's business involved him in a variety of Christian ministries, churches, and parachurch organizations. After years of seeing behind the scenes, of being in the boardrooms, of looking at the spreadsheets, of listening to the aspirations of would-be Christian leaders, he had to make a conscious effort not to become cynical. So much of what he heard and saw and read was for the personal promotion and self-advancement of those who masked their agendas in pious platitudes and spiritual clichés, raising money for the "kingdom of God" while they took a 10 percent commission.

But when we get to Heaven, there will be . . .

no hidden agendas,
no ulterior motives,
no secret ambitions,
no selfish pride.

Everyone—*every single person*—will live and serve for the praise and glory of God's only Son, Jesus Christ! And as you and I enter our heavenly home, we will have the indescribable joy of laying at our Lord's nail-pierced feet any glory and honor we have received.

There will be no painful comparisons and no sibling rivalry. Every relationship will be reconciled and restored. Can you imagine? There will be . . .

humility and harmony,
love and laughter,
peace and joy,
silence and singing,
kindness and thoughtfulness,
unity and purity,
contentment and consideration.

One day our heavenly home will be ready. With loving eagerness and anticipation of our joy, the Father will open the door to His House and gather His children home.

For the past several years, my husband and I, along

with our family, have celebrated Thanksgiving at my father's house. My sweet sister-in-law, Jane Austin, who is Franklin's wife and one of my dearest friends, does most of the cooking. The meal is always abundant and delicious—turkey with dressing and gravy, ham, green beans, corn pudding, two kinds of sweet potato casseroles, sticky rice, two kinds of cranberry relish, fruit ambrosia, yeast rolls, pumpkin and apple and mincemeat pies with real whipped cream, sweet iced tea . . . my mouth waters just thinking about it! But the highlight of Thanksgiving is not the food, or the televised football games, or the fun. The highlight is always the fellowship around the dining room table. As we sip our coffee and gorge on one last piece of pie, my father presides at the head of the table as each person shares what he or she is most thankful for. Most of us, including the ruggedly handsome boys who are crossing the threshold into manhood, have tears in our eyes as we listen to the testimonies of thanksgiving to God for His faithfulness and goodness throughout the previous year. As I drink in my father's love and my mother's radiance and my brother's strength and my sister-in-law's misty-eyed joy and my entire family's gratitude to God, again and again I have exclaimed in my heart, "It just doesn't get any better than this!" *But it will!*

One day, in My Father's House, the table will be set and supper will be ready.[10] One day you and I and all of the Father's children will be seated around that table. One day our Father will preside as He gathers us to Himself, listening intently and lovingly as we share our love for each other and our love for Him.[11] One day My Father's House will be filled with His family, and it won't get any better than that! *Ever!* That will be Heaven for me!

A Home
You Are Invited
to Claim As Your Own

The invitation to My Father's House
is extended to all,
but you have to RSVP.

The Spirit and the bride say, "Come!"
And let him who hears say,
"Come!"
—REVELATION 22:17

My Father's House is a home in Heaven . . .

    . . . it's the home of your dreams,

        . . . it's a home that is safe,

            . . . it's a home you can never lose,

                . . . it's a home of lasting value,

                    . . . it's a home that's been paid for,

                        . . . it's a home filled with family,

and, best of all, it's a home you are invited to claim as your own! Heaven is the inheritance of God's children.

News media will often announce the deaths of the extremely wealthy along with estimates of their estates. Invariably, a follow-up article will appear within a few days, detailing the fights and lawsuits breaking out among potential heirs over their perceived inheritance. One very wealthy woman's estate was pilfered by her butler. A deceased billionaire's carefully hoarded lifetime of treasures was snatched away from his children by his mistress. An eccentric multimillionaire left her entire estate to her dogs! The stories go on and on.

The apostle Peter confirms that the inheritance being laid up for the Father's children "can never perish, spoil or fade"—it is "kept in heaven for you" (1 Peter 1:4). Although our inheritance is safely stored in heaven, there is a condition we have to meet before we can claim it: "He who overcomes will inherit all this, and I will be his God and he will be my son" (Rev. 21:7).

What do you have to *overcome* in order to claim My Father's House as your own?

You have to overcome your pride that refuses to acknowledge you are a sinner who needs a Savior.

You have to overcome your pride that insists if you do more good works than bad works, God will let you inside His heavenly home.

You have to overcome your unbelief that Jesus Christ is God's Son, the sinner's Savior, the captive's Ransom, *and the only way to Heaven.*

You have to overcome your religiosity that substitutes positive thinking for holiness, rituals for repentance, traditions for truth, and orthodoxy for obedience.

As much as John may have recoiled from marring

his glorious vision with anything unpleasant, he remained true to the directive he had received. He related very honestly that while there will be those who will live inside of Heaven, there will also be those who live outside.

It's Your Choice to Go to Heaven

Two places are being prepared in the universe at this moment. One is Heaven, which is being prepared for the Lord to live in forever with His loved ones. The other place is hell, which is being prepared for the devil, his demons, and all those who refuse God's gracious offer of salvation through His Son, Jesus Christ. John was very clear as he stated that "the cowardly, the unbelieving, the vile, the murderers, the sexually immoral, those who practice magic arts, the idolaters and all liars—their place will be in the fiery lake of burning sulfur. This is the second death" (Rev. 21:8). In the event someone is not paying attention, and because this is so serious, John repeats the warning, "Outside are the dogs, those who practice magic arts, the sexually immoral, the murderers, the idolaters and everyone who loves and practices falsehood."[1]

In order to more fully comprehend John's words, consider for a moment the contrast between the two places:

Heaven is a home where there is no more suffering or death or mourning or crying or pain.[2]

Hell is a hole where there is great suffering and weeping and gnashing of teeth.[3] (The only time I gnashed my teeth was in childbirth when the pain became totally unbearable!)

Heaven is a home where there is absolute safety and eternal security within the high, thick walls.[4]

Hell is a hole that is described as the Abyss, or a bottomless pit.[5] Those who fall into it will have the sensation of never being secure, of always being in danger.

Heaven is a home that is stable, unshakable, and unmovable with twelve foundations.[6]

Hell is a hole that undulates and changes like the unstable surface of a lake.[7]

Heaven is a home in which there is no more night or darkness.[8]

Hell is a hole of total darkness where the sun never rises and the light never comes.[9] (Have you heard people say they want to go to hell so they can be with their friends? Well, their friends may be there, but they will never see them because it's totally dark.)

Heaven is a home where the kings of the nations of the earth bring their glory and where God's children gather to worship Him forever and ever.[10]

Hell is a hole whose inhabitants live in eternal solitary confinement with nothing to distract them from their own misery, greed, selfishness, anger, hate, pride, cruelty, and godlessness.[11]

Heaven is a home where the river of life flows continuously, bringing fruit for the healing of the nations.[12]

Hell is a hole filled with fire creating unending thirst, torment, and burning dissatisfaction.[13]

Heaven is a home where we will serve God and see His face.[14]

Hell is a hole that will be totally devoid of God's presence. Those who exist there will know they were created for God yet will be separated from Him forever.[15]

Praise God! I've been saved from hell, and I'm going to Heaven! I've made the choice! God doesn't technically send anyone to hell. A person only goes to hell by his or her own free choice, which is automatically made when he or she refuses God's escape plan—His gracious provision of Jesus Christ as our Savior.[16]

Some people may think this sounds narrow-minded, exclusive, unfair, and intolerant. But that person is overlooking the fact that God is not arbitrary or whimsical. He extends to all His generous invitation to claim His House as our eternal home. If we accept His invitation, we live with Him forever. However, if we do not accept because we refuse His only Son as our Savior, then *we exclude ourselves* from My Father's House. It's our choice.

It's Your Choice to Be His Child

My Heavenly Father's House is not for everyone, just as my earthly father's house is not for everyone. The place I call home in western North Carolina is secured by a tall fence, guarded by dogs, and situated on a mountain accessible only by a narrow, winding road. While many thousands of people have expressed interest in seeing it, it is off-limits to the general public. Only members of the family or specially invited guests are allowed to visit.

Suppose someone decided to challenge the privacy of my earthly father's house. That person would drive up the winding mountain road only to be stopped by a gate that is situated in a high fence. He or she could bang on the gate, and yell insistently, or cry pitifully, "Billy Graham, let me in. I've watched you on TV. I've read your books. I've attended your crusades. I've even supported your ministry financially. You owe it to me to let me come in." But my father would say, in essence, "Depart from me. I don't know you."

On the other hand, if I drive up that same narrow, winding lane and come to the same closed gate, I would call, "Daddy, this is Anne. I've come home. Let me in." And the gate would swing wide open. Do you know why? *Because I'm the father's child!*

Are you confident that you will be accepted when you stand at the gate to My Father's House? Since Heaven is off-limits to the general public, are you assured that when you step into eternity, Heaven's gate will be opened wide because you are the Father's child? Or will you be like those people Jesus described who would try to just "show up," expecting to be admitted and saying to Him, "'Lord, Lord, did we not prophesy in your name, and in your name drive out demons and perform many miracles?' Then I will tell them plainly, 'I never knew you. Away from me, you evildoers!'"[17]

In His response to the would-be heavenly gate-crashers, Jesus described many people who prophesied, who quoted Scripture and perhaps even taught Scripture, as *evildoers*. He described many who drove out demons, who got involved in service and religious activities, as *evildoers*. In His own language, He said many people who performed miracles, who even seemingly received answers to prayer, were *evildoers*! Evildoers may have been religious in their lifetimes, but they never established a personal relationship with God through faith in Jesus Christ! *Evildoers are those who never knew Christ!*

These evildoers will be kept outside and denied entrance into Heaven along with the cowardly, who cared more about what others thought of them than what God thought, and the "unbelieving," who refused to believe that Jesus Christ is the way, the truth, and the life and that no one enters Heaven except through faith in Him.[18] Standing outside Heaven will also be the vile; the murderers; the sexually immoral who called their behavior "fooling around" or "an alternate lifestyle" or "safe-sex"; those who practiced the magic arts of the New Age as well as Wicca and the old witchcraft; the idolaters who sold their health, their families, their relationships, their integrity, their character, and their very souls for material possessions; and all liars (see Rev. 21:8).

Make no mistake about it! Heaven is a home populated by the Lord and His loved ones who have made the deliberate choice to be there. But there will also be those who will be outside. By their own choice! Based on the choices you have made, if you were to die today, would you be inside *or outside* of Heaven's gates?[19]

Are you troubled because you have made some bad choices and the life you used to lead is in that descriptive list of "outsiders"? In his letter to the Corinthian church, the apostle Paul emphatically affirmed the exclusion of certain offenders from My Father's House. With ringing clarity, he challenged, "Do you not know that the wicked will not inherit the kingdom of God? Do not be deceived: Neither the sexually immoral nor idolators nor adulterers nor male prostitutes nor homosexual offenders nor thieves nor the greedy nor drunkards nor slanderers nor swindlers will inherit the kingdom of God." But then Paul gives the glorious acknowledgment, "And that is what some of you *were*. But you were washed, you were sanctified, you were justified in the name of the Lord Jesus Christ and by the Spirit of our God."[20]

Praise God! The invitation to come into My Father's House has been extended to *everyone* through Jesus Christ at the Cross. BUT . . . when the invitation is refused, the door to Heaven is closed. "Nothing impure will ever enter it, nor will anyone who does what is shameful or deceitful, but only those whose names are written in the Lamb's book of life" (Rev. 21:27).

How can you know for sure that your name is written in the Lamb's book of life and you are therefore a child of God, recognized and accepted by the Heavenly Father? How can you know for sure that Heaven is your home?

It's Your Choice to Place Your Faith in Him

The beauty of this assurance of acceptance by God is illustrated by the true story of a little boy, years ago, who lived in London, England. He heard that D. L. Moody was coming to preach, and on the day of the meeting, the little boy walked across the city to hear the famous American evangelist. When he drew near to the church, he saw that it was situated on a hill.

The sun was setting, and the colors of the sunset were reflected in the multifaceted stained-glass windows, making them look as though they were glowing. The sound of hundreds of voices undergirded by a powerful pipe organ drifted toward him. He forgot how tired he was, and he ran all the way up the long granite staircase that led to the front door.

As he reached the threshold and was ready to open the door to enter, a big hand grasped him firmly by the shoulder and spun him around. "What do you think you're doing, laddie?" demanded a tall, severe-looking deacon.

The little boy told him he had traveled all the way across the city in order to hear Mr. Moody, and he wanted to go inside. The keeper of the door looked the little boy up and down from head to toe, taking in the uncombed hair, the unwashed face, the unshod feet, and the unclean clothes. He then retorted, "Not you, sonny. You're too dirty to go inside. Be gone."

The little boy just stuck his nose up in the air and determined to find another way inside the church. But the other doors were locked, and the windows were too high to climb through. Dejected, he went back to the front steps, plopped down, and began to cry.

113

Just then he was distracted by a carriage that pulled up to the foot of the steps. Out bounded a distinguished-looking gentleman who marched quickly up the steps. He stopped when he came to the little boy, noticing his grimy, tear-streaked face. "What's the matter, boy?" he inquired. The little boy explained, and the gentleman looked at him kindly then extended his hand. "Here. Put your hand in mine." The boy thought about it for a moment, then he slipped his little hand into the big man's grasp. Hand in hand they walked up the steps of the church. When they came to the door that had previously been shut to the little boy, it was flung wide open. Hand in hand the big man and the little street urchin walked down the center aisle. When they came to the front row, the gentleman deposited the boy on the pew then walked up to the platform, into the pulpit and began to preach. The man was Mr. D. L. Moody!

The only way the little boy got inside that church was because he was holding Mr. Moody's hand. In the same way, the only reason *anyone*—you

or I

or Billy Graham

or Pope John Paul

or Mother Teresa

or a murderer on death row

or an alcoholic in the gutter—

the only reason *anyone* gets into Heaven is because that person is holding the hand of Jesus. He extends it to you and to me and to the whole world at the Cross. And He invites us to come with Him into My Father's House.

When have you deliberately placed your hand of faith in the hand of Jesus by claiming His death as the sacrifice for your own sin, asking Him to forgive you, giving Him the controlling authority in your life—for the rest of your life? If you have never taken His hand, or if you are not sure you have, would you pray a simple prayer, something like this:

> *Dear God,*
>
> *I want to become a member of Your family. I want to know for sure that You are my Father and I am Your child. I want my name recorded in the Lamb's book of life. So right now, I accept Your invitation to claim You as my Father and Your home as my own by confessing to You that I am a sinner. I'm*

sorry for my sin and I'm willing to turn from it, but I need Your help. I believe that Jesus died on the Cross to take away my sin, and I believe Jesus rose up from the dead to give me eternal life. I open up my life and invite Jesus to come in and take full control. From this moment forward, I will live my life for Him.

I now place my hand in His.

Amen.

The moment you take His hand by faith, claiming His home as your own, you can look forward, even in troubled times . . . *with hope!* [21]

Because your name is now written in the Lamb's book of life, never to be erased!

Because this world is not your home.

Because death does not have the final word.

Because failure is not final.

Because one day your faith will become sight and you will see the gates of pearl flung open for you.

Because, BEST OF ALL, you will see God's face and hear God's voice say, *"Welcome to your Father's House!"*

He's Left the Light on ...
for You

✨

Your Father is waiting
to welcome you home—unconditionally!

So he got up and went to his father.
    But while he was still a long way off,
his father saw him
    and was filled with compassion for him;
he ran to his son,
    threw his arms around him and kissed him.
                              —LUKE 15:20

I recently drove home to my father's house. Night fell as I entered the Blue Ridge Mountains and began the last leg of my four-hour drive. When I rolled down the car windows, felt the cool mountain air, smelled the damp, pungent earth, and heard the night song of the crickets, my anticipation intensified. As I rounded the last bend in the road, my eyes began to strain as I peered through the darkness. I was looking for one thing—the lantern that dangles from an old birdhouse by the driveway. Would the light be on to welcome me home? It was!

And God the Father has left the light on in Heaven to welcome you and me home! When the apostle John saw My Father's House, "it shone with the glory of God. . . . The city does not need the sun or the moon to shine on it, for the glory of God gives it light, and the Lamb is its lamp . . . for there will be no night there" (Rev. 21:11, 23, 25). If you have RSVPed to the Father's invitation to be His child and therefore, one day, to share His House, then He is waiting to welcome you home.

There are those who believe if we die when we are failing miserably, or when we are out of fellowship with the Father, or when in some way we are not living a life that is worthy of our Family name, then we will not be welcomed into Heaven. In other words, if we arrive in the "dark," the light of the Father's welcome will not be left on for us.

Following this line of thinking, if a person commits suicide, even though he or she had previously taken Jesus Christ by faith as Savior and Lord, that person would no longer be welcome in Heaven. I disagree. If one of my children ran from a problem he should have faced, or quit a project he should have finished, or for any reason whatsoever showed up unexpectedly at my door, I would still welcome him. Because this is his home and he is my child.

I once heard my sister acknowledge that she has made several wrong choices in her life. After one particularly devastating decision, she said, she drove up to our parents' mountain home. As she neared the winding mountain driveway, she became terrified of facing our father. How would he react? What would he say? Would he even speak to her or be willing to see her at all? When she pulled into the driveway at the side of the house, she saw him standing at the door. As she got out of her car with trembling legs and pounding heart, she rejoiced to see him throw his arms open wide and then to hear him say, "Welcome *home!*"

Praise God! *Praise God! PRAISE GOD! **PRAISE GOD!*** We can do nothing to earn our heavenly home, and therefore we can do nothing to lose it! The gates are open wide to all who simply accept His invitation to enter by faith through the Cross of His Son, Jesus Christ. The Father is eagerly waiting for His children to come home! And the welcome He extends is unconditional!

He has left the light on—*for you!*

Notes

Looking Forward to Heaven
1. (page 3) See Hebrews 9:27.

A Home in Heaven
1. (page 16) John 14:2–3.
2. (page 16) 1 Corinthians 2:9.
3. (page 22) Genesis 2:8–9.
4. (page 23) John 14:2.

The Home of Your Dreams
1. (page 34) John 8:12.
2. (page 34) Matthew 5:14.

A Home That Is Safe
1. (page 46) John 3:16.
2. (page 47) Dr. Henry Morris, *The Revelation Record* (Carol Stream, Ill.: Tyndale, 1983), 450–51.
3. (page 48) See John 14:2–3.
4. (page 50) See 1 Corinthians 2:9.

A Home You Can Never Lose
1. (page 60) See Matthew 6:19–20.
2. (page 61) Hebrews 11:8–10.
3. (page 61) See Hebrews 11:13.

A Home of Lasting Value
1. (page 69) See Matthew 6:19–20.

2. (page 74) See 2 Peter 1:11 and 1 Corinthians 3:10–15.

3. (page 75) See 1 John 3:2.

4. (page 76) See 2 Corinthians 3:18 and Romans 8:29.

5. (page 76) See 1 Peter 1:6–7.

6. (page 77) See Ephesians 4:20–24.

7. (page 77) See Hebrews 5:7–8.

8. (page 78) See Romans 8:28.

9. (page 78) See John 17:6, 24.

A Home That's Paid For

1. (page 83) See Revelation 13:8; Matthew 25:34.

A Home Filled with Family

1. (page 90) See Leviticus 16.

2. (page 90) Hebrews 10:19–20.

3. (page 93) See 1 Thessalonians 4:13.

4. (page 93) Often the question is raised, "Will I recognize my loved ones in Heaven?" The answer is yes. The Bible tells us that when we get to Heaven we will have bodies like the one Jesus had after the resurrection (see Phil. 3:21). After His resurrection, Jesus was physically recognizable (see Luke 24:31). His disciples were able to examine the scars on His hands and feet where the nails from His crucifixion had been (see John 20:20, 24–27). He ate fish (see Luke 24:41–43). In other words, His body was a physical body of flesh and bones that had been familiar to His disciples during His three years of public ministry, yet after the resurrection it was also uniquely suited to live in eternity (see

Luke 24:37–39 and Acts 1:9–11).

5. (page 93) See 1 Thessalonians 4:18.

6. (page 93) While there may have been a time in the past when this would be true, today this comment is made totally in jest. I love, respect, and enjoy my brother.

7. (page 94) See 1 John 3:2.

8. (page 94) See Genesis 18:25.

9. (page 94) See Luke 23:32–43.

10. (page 99) See Revelation 19:9.

11. (page 99) See Revelation 19:5.

A Home You Are Invited to Claim As Your Own

1. (page 105) Revelation 22:15.

2. (page 105) See Revelation 21:4.

3. (page 105) See Matthew 13:50.

4. (page 105) See Revelation 21:12, 17.

5. (page 105) See Revelation 20:3.

6. (page 106) See Revelation 21:14.

7. (page 106) See Revelation 20:10.

8. (page 106) See Revelation 21:25.

9. (page 106) See Matthew 25:30.

10. (page 106) See Revelation 21:24.

11. (page 106) The following verses indicate that there will be people cast into hell together. However, the physical darkness and torment are so all-consuming and individualized, it will be as though each one is isolated in his or her own agony: Luke 13:28; 16:19–31; Revelation 20:10, 15.

12. (page 106) See Revelation 22:1–2.

13. (page 106) See Revelation 20:15.

14. (page 106) See Revelation 22:4.

15. (page 107) See Matthew 7:23.

16. (page 107) See John 3:16–18.

17. (page 109) Matthew 7:22–23.

18. (page 110) See John 14:6.

19. (page 110) Please keep in mind that a choice not to deliberately, consciously respond to God's invitation to receive Jesus Christ as your personal Savior is considered by God as a choice to reject Him and therefore puts you outside of Heaven in eternity.

20. (page 111) 1 Corinthians 6:9–11. Emphasis mine.

21. (page 116) Have you taken God's "hand" in prayer, confessed your sin, claimed Jesus as your Savior, yet still doubt that Heaven is your home? If so, I would suggest you pray this prayer for the *last time*—but this time pray by faith in God's Word.

    God's Word says that if you confess your sin, "he is faithful and just and will forgive us our sins and purify us from all unrighteousness" (1 John 1:9). In response, faith says, "Thank You. I have confessed my sin; therefore I believe You have forgiven me."

    God's Word says that if you receive Jesus and believe in Him, He gives you "the right to become children of God" (John 1:12). In response, faith says, "Thank You. I am now Your child."

    God's Word says that if you place your faith in Jesus

Christ, you "shall not perish but have eternal life" (John 3:16). In response, faith says, "Thank You. I have placed my faith in Jesus, and therefore I have eternal life—I now know Heaven is mine."

Take God at His Word. Do not pray this prayer depending on your feelings. Saving faith is an act of your will to choose to take God at His Word. The assurance of your salvation and rebirth into His family will come as you begin, every day, to pray, read your Bible, and live your life in obedience and service to Him.